JUST

START

FIVE A'S TOWARD OVERCOMING FEAR

VARIAN D. HARRIS

Just Start: Five A's to Overcoming Fear

Copyright © 2023 by Varian D. Harris

Transformational Leader | Speaker | Marketplace Influencer
www.VarianHarris.com
info@varianharris.com

Zyia Christian Publishing, LLC
zyiachristianpublising@gmail.com

Text Design by: Nyisha D. Davis

ISBN: 979-8-218-17193-3

Distruibuted by IngramSpark.

Printed in the United States of America.

10 9 8 7 6 5 4 3 2 1

About the Author

Transformational Leader | Speaker | Marketplace Influencer

Varian D. Harris is a faith-based leader in the community of Atlanta, Georgia, where he resides. He is the President of Omnikey Christian University and holds a Bachelor of Arts in Leadership and Administration from Beulah Heights University and a Master's Degree in Christian Ministry from Liberty University. He is currently pursuing his Ph.D. in Transformative Leadership and an Honorary Doctorate from Heart Bible International University of Doctorate in Education and Leadership in Ministry.

Varian is intentionally blurring the lines between faith-based industry and the marketplace. He is an up-and-coming transformational leader with an entrepreneurial mastermind passionate about transforming communities and helping people grow in their purpose. Varian speaks to people's hearts, inspiring them to discover and activate their God-given gifts. Varian believes everyone is born with a gift to serve humanity. His gift is to be a spokesperson for the underserved and underprivileged community.

info@varianharris.com
www.VarianHarris.com

CONTENT

INTRODUCTION

In today's society, millions of people are hungry for success. They try to find multiple streams of income as a way to attain success. However, the real solution is understanding their passion. Understanding your passion will drive you toward success, but the 'fear of beginning' can hinder you from reaching your goal. Question... How do you define fear?

You must realize that fear is just an imagination. We all have a sense of fear that could cause us to quit, give up on our purpose, or even hinder us from leaping toward our purpose. Are you gripped in a place of fear that prevents you from taking off? If you don't take the time to deal with your fear, it will overcome your dream.

Every day, people strive to move beyond their limitations. They have everything planned out, they see the vision clearly, and some even have the strategy to move. But the fear in them hinders them from taking off.

If you see this as yourself, why don't you move forward? Why remain normal when God has called you to be abnormal? What's really holding you back? Only you can take this moment and discover the reason for your why's and take action to move forward in life.

I'm here to assist you in the paths I took to face my 'fear of beginning'. Was it easy? No. Challenging? Yes, to the point that even today, I checked my confidence and evaluated the cause of my hesitation to move forward.

Sometimes in life, we prey or pry on looking successful, which keeps us from moving forward in our divine purpose. One of the biggest giants in this area that we have to overcome is social media. It has not only kept us from being honest with ourselves, but has kept us from personally socializing with the truth aspect of life.

Everything is a picture for likes, hearts and cash. So, how can someone be true and truly understand their mental and social problems? We encounter challenges to keep this act going, and we lose the very essence of who we are and what we are purposed for in life.

I'm a prime example of this new age model; I wanted to portray that my life "is" good. However, I had to learn that the key to everything is understanding how to move toward excellence. I never thought I would be the person to deal with fear. Yet, alone be the one who would be afraid of a challenge. Why?

Throughout my life, especially in my teenage years, I have always been a bold person to be the first to try something new and be the first person to volunteer for anything; acting, singing, speaking and playing instruments. I would do it because a need needed to be handled. I thought, "Who had time to wait on people who were shy to respond? Either you're going to do it or not." That was my philosophy.

Until I was hit with failing the standardized test of science portion in high school, I was always bold and stood for the test of time. Every quarter, I failed by three to four points. I saw my peers moving forward and progressing, and I was stuck. I begin to think; Like, am I the problem? Am I not smart enough? Am I really a failure? This is all happening during the time I received a scholarship and my college acceptance letter as I prepared for college.

The time had come to graduate, and I received a letter from the Board of Education. They declared that if I did not pass the Standardized Test of Science, I could not graduate, even with me having a GPA of 3.75 and receiving a certificate of completion for all grade levels. I felt worse. My confidence dropped to its lowest.

It wasn't until I was married ten years later that I understood that my life was in a spiral of feeling defeated, even when I had accomplished so much. This feeling of defeat resided in me. I felt destroyed and was afraid of moving forward in life. I never want anyone to remain in the place that I was in, which is this book's purpose.

As I walk you through this journey, you will have moments to write and reflect on the times you felt disappointed and fearful. You will also discover useful tools and the wisdom to apply them to overcome your fear. We will cover five steps that will help you overcome your fear. I call them the Five A's; acknowledging you are in a fearful stage, accepting that you are in fear, analyzing your fear, announcing your fear, and seeing the accomplishment of being out of fear. After reading this book, you will know how to take the first vital step toward achieving your dreams. You will overcome all limitations and **Just Start**. Let's Start!

A Fearless Vision

The thrill and joy of doing something you love with an estimated end goal of success is a wonderful thing. However, the fear of failure could hold you back. Whether you serve as a minister, leader or entrepreneur, you are still susceptible to fear and the dangers of fear becoming a hindrance to success. It doesn't matter what fear you are facing in your life; there is always hope for overcoming it through discipline, work and dedication.

Fear is a normal human experience that can pop up at any time. It's helpful to know that fear is completely natural and normal. It's important to recognize fear for what it is—a feeling of apprehension, tension, or unease about something that may or may not happen in the future. Fear is real and has to be overcome with action.

Fear can be better understood when it's defined as:
- A feeling of unease about an impending event or experience.
- A warning signal telling you to avoid danger.
- Stems from uncertainty, which means that overcoming fear requires approaching the unknown with faith and confidence.

Scripture tells us:
- To trust God in every area of your life. (Psalm 146:3)
- God will never leave you nor forsake you; have the effect of making you feel invincible, like nothing can stand in your way. (Hebrews 13:5, Deuteronomy 31:6)
- God will give you strength when you are weak. (2 Corinthians 12:9)

Fear can be a paralyzing emotion that takes over our lives and keeps us from achieving the things we want to do. But by recognizing those fears and taking steps to address them head-on, we can begin to gain control over our lives. By taking action and accomplishing something, no matter how small it may seem, we can start to rebuild our confidence and increase the number of assets in our life.

As Christians, we also have the Hope of Jesus that gives us strength and courage to keep going, even when facing difficult challenges. He will provide us with opportunities to continue growing and strengthening our faith. When we keep Jesus at the center of our lives, He will give us the power to move forward and experience life in a more meaningful way. So, if you are feeling overwhelmed by fear, remember that there is always hope through Jesus, and you can take action toward your goals. With God's help, you can build an impressive list of assets in your life and be free from fear!

By following Jesus' example, you start to recognize your fears and take steps to overcome them. Whether it means facing them head-on or stepping out into something new, He will be right there with you every step of the way. With Christ as your strength and guide, you will be able to accomplish great things and create valuable assets for yourself.

Maybe you'd like to start a business, learn a new skill, or volunteer at an organization that is doing something you believe in. As Jesus guides your every step, amazing accomplishments are within reach! Take the first step with courage and determination and watch how your life blossoms in unexpected ways. Life may have its challenges, but it doesn't have to be lived fearfully. Instead, live with hope through Jesus Christ.

We all struggle with fear from time to time. But, remember that God can help us overcome it every day if we choose to follow Him.

He is the source of our strength, our courage and our hope. Take that first step forward today and trust in the Lord, who will be with you every step of the way. Embrace your fears and have faith that God will lead you to a future full of peace, joy, love, and opportunity. With Jesus by your side, there is nothing you can't do!

Many amazing things can happen when we are brave enough to face our fears by living life intentionally with Jesus at its center. Not only on the inside, but also in tangible form within our lives; unused abilities become put into action, leading to personal growth and development, as well as creating powerful assets like job skills or business opportunities. Each experience brings us one step closer to our destiny, and when we have faith in Jesus, the possibilities are endless.

No matter what life throws your way, never forget that you can conquer anything with Jesus by your side. Waiting for the perfect moment to take action or worrying about an uncertain outcome will only keep you from achieving what God has promised for you. So, start small and build on it. Each victory will lead to greater success down the road.

Take courage, knowing that whatever path you choose, Jesus is there to help you overcome fear and walk in faith toward a better tomorrow! When circumstances seem daunting, stay focused on why you're doing this, and remember that God always provides an opportunity for growth, no matter how hard it may be. With Him as our source of strength, we can take on any challenge that comes our way.

As you strive to build assets and create a better life for yourself, allow Jesus to be your light in the darkness and your anchor in tumultuous weather. His promises will never fail, and He will always provide the wisdom to make sound decisions. So, whether it's making the right career choice or investing wisely, let Him lead you forward.

God has given us wonderful gifts: courage, resilience, and determination—which is all essential ingredients for success. As you face fear head-on with these tools under your belt, remember God's promise of hope and grace during times of suffering. With His hand guiding yours, nothing is impossible. Take a leap of faith and trust the direction He's leading you.

It's not always easy. However, through each accomplishment, your faith will be strengthened and your fear replaced with hope. Accomplishments that generate assets in your life can open up new doors of opportunity, as well as give you a sense of control over any potential obstacles that may arise. With Jesus always at your side, never let fear keep you from achieving great things. Trust His word and have faith that whatever path you choose will lead to growth and success!

Don't allow fear to stop you from fulfilling your full potential. When you don't attain your goals, your path, and the paths of many lives that would have been affected by your progress, remains uncertain. Fear does not have to be a barrier; it can be an effective tool to clarify your path.

Successful people don't reach their goals because of the absence of fear. They have methods to effectively manage and get rid of fear. I hope you embrace the five steps to overcoming your fear and reaching your goals, as discussed in this book.

Let Us Pray!

Oh Lord,

We come to You in prayer today, asking for Your help and guidance. We are struggling with fear and anxiety that seem so overwhelming at times.

Help us remember that You have promised never to leave or forsake us, no matter our challenges.

Remind us of Your goodness and mercy when our thoughts become clouded by worry. Fill our hearts with courage and strength to overcome the fears that stand in our way.

In moments of darkness, let us confidently turn to You, knowing that You will light up our paths. Help us to trust in Your timing and plan as we take steps forward in faith.

We thank You for always being present in our lives even when it feels like everything else is crumbling around us.

Forgive us for not trusting in You and doubting Your power to help us get through our worries and fears. We praise you, Lord, for being a shelter in the time of storm and a rock that never fails us. Amen.

$\mathscr{S}tep$ 1
ACKNOWLEDGEMENT

On your mark. Get set. Go! This phrase expresses the mental drive when a visionary has an idea that will bring them closer to a level of success. Sometimes as visionaries, we wonder why we hesitate to move forward. We think from the end in mind rather than from the beginning stage. The scripture says, don't despise small beginnings. (Zechariah 4:10 NLT) Your beginning is not a small thing. The longevity of understanding the process from beginning to end will work for your good. Yes, you will have the following questions. Will I fail in the process? Will it come out the way I saw it in my head? However, it is your responsibility not to despise your beginning.

As leaders, we must understand that every vision has to go through its process. And with every vision, the visionary must also understand they must go through a process. It's the process that challenges us to grow from within and see the outcome of life for our success. Don't despise small beginnings. You may be asking yourself, How can I see this scripture in play when I, as a visionary, always see the big picture? Visionary thrives off of making a vision a reality. The key to this is seeing it through, one step at a time. One major hiccup is feeling like a failure and walking in fear when the vision or the process of the vision doesn't line up with the timeline or what you see in your head.

Man, I wish I could tell you about all the mistakes I made in trying to make sure that God's vision manifested in the way that I saw it. I spent countless hours and money pushing a vision that the timing played a major part in my movement—noticing and understanding that even the timing is important. We have to remind ourselves not to get complacent in waiting that we let procrastination hinder and cripple us toward fear that we don't move.

This brings us to the awareness of acknowledging our short-comings. Acknowledging is the first key to understanding where we are in our faith walk. You may ask yourself, why do I have to acknowledge my shortcomings? How can someone cross through a desert if they do not have a map to discover where they are located? It's all in the process of finding your location and taking one step at a time.

Let's take it a little deeper. Acknowledgment, by definition is "an act of accepting that something exists or is true, or that something is there".[1] I like to call this self-awareness. Acknowledging what is true and accepting who you are (your purpose, strengths, AND weaknesses) is the most powerful step to your Just Start Journey. The challenge is usually that when we acknowledge a person, place, thing, value, idea, or quality, we can quickly label and judge it as "good" or "bad". The focus right now is to simply acknowledge what is true about you and your fear and let it be.

A great way to pinpoint who you truly are and what your fear is is to simply write it down. Find a serene place to sit and gather your thoughts on the matter. You must reach into your feelings and emotions for this to work. Ensure there are no distractions what-soever. With a pen and notepad, write down specific thoughts that come up when you think about how you truly are, and list the root

---

1 Psychalive.org. (2023).

cause of your fear.

After addressing the elephant in the room, it's time to identify your purpose. Now that you have admitted your fears, you can turn them into courage. Now that you see the hurdle in your way, you can brace yourself to jump over it by reminding yourself of why you're on this journey to success. Your why must be bigger than your fear, or the hurdle will look too intimidating and impossible to scale. Your fear can only have dominion over you if you let it. Taking action to succeed despite its existence will help you achieve your desires. You will feel more empowered to approach your fears when you acknowledge them and remind yourself how powerful your determination is.

With this journal entry, you have 2 Parts!

1. Going to https://enneagram.bz/en to complete the Enneagram personality test. This simple personality test not only identifies some fears and desires, but also can help shed light on some of your subconscious motivations that influence your emotions, attitudes, and behavior.

2. Complete the Enneagram and then answer the questions below.

Journal your answers:
- What were your results from the Enneagram test?
- Did it resonate with your thoughts and feelings about your self and those around you? What core fear or belief did you identify?
- How did this fear develop?

JOURNAL

Now that you have acknowledged your fear, take time to reframe the false belief by listing what is true despite that fear. Were you able to connect with those truths? If so, why or why not?

Let Us Pray!!

Heavenly Father,

We come before You today with reverence to You in our hearts. We acknowledge the power and presence of fear in our lives and how it shapes our thoughts and emotions. In moments of uncertainty or discomfort, we know that fear can be a difficult emotion to manage.

But even as we turn to You for help, we remember that You are ultimately in control. Help us to take refuge in Your perfect love and protection so that when we feel overwhelmed by worry or anxiety, we can find strength and hope through trust in You. Let us not give up hope, but instead choose faith over doubt and courage over timidity.

Give us the grace to move forward despite whatever fears may stand against us. Let us cling to the promises of Your Word, knowing that You have gone before us. Comfort us when we fear and help us to live a life of faithfulness—in small steps and big leaps.

We thank You for Your love, presence, and protection as we face our fears. Amen.

Step 2

ACCEPTANCE

One truth about fear is that it never goes away unless you confront it. Fear you don't deal with for a year will be right where you left it. This fear will remain a hindrance to your progress for as long as it is not confronted. Although you've acknowledged your fear, you can still be ashamed and embarrassed about it. It doesn't matter how rich, strong or intelligent you are, fear can still affect you.

The key to breaking out is learning to accept your fear. Blaming others for your inability to start a project will not help you confront your fears; gaining ownership will. The solution is not in someone else's words, actions or deeds. It is in your responsibility. How can you gain ownership and conquer fear?

Have you ever questioned if you are doing the right thing? I have many times! I remember back in my junior year of high school when I was one of the top linemen on the football team. During my senior year, I decided to quit football and pursue music. I felt the pull to do something different. See, in my family, and we didn't just sing; we SANG. My family has always had vocals that we sang in church. I realized I had a great desire for music, and I had the vocals to pursue it.

However, many did not agree with my choice. When I finally mustered up the courage to tell my parents I was pursuing band and chorus, I was met face-to-face with rejection and criticism that made me question my life choices up to that point. I was hurt and ashamed, because I wanted support from my family and approval from my dad. Despite my family, I pursued my interest in music, and with time my passion grew like wildfire!

I learned to express myself and connect with others around me through the art of music. I finally felt SEEN! Music unlocked my mind and interest that I never knew I had. I was able to accept that even though I feared rejection. I could accept myself and the gifts that God had given me instead of focusing on something that did not cultivate joy in my life.

As you know, acceptance means to approve of or take responsibility for something or someone. Therefore, once the individual has acknowledged their fears and doubts by understanding the root, there can be acceptance to understand what the needs are to quiet the fears and lessen the doubt.

Take the time to silence your fears by utilizing the instructions and questions below:

- Name the fear or doubt.
- What do you think is the root cause of this fear or doubt?
- Is this fear valid? Why or why not?
- If this fear is valid, take time to assess and accept what you need or what shift is needed that could help dissolve the doubt and fear.
- Do you know someone right now who can support you or help you solve your problem?
- Is there a boundary you need to put in place for yourself or others to lessen your doubts?

As we dive into this particular step of accepting our fear, we must consider how we arrive at this part of our life where fear has gripped us to remain immovable.

- What are the key things that got you here?
- Why is it hard for you to embrace the hiccups of your challenges?
- Is it that you are blaming others and not yourself?

Let's look over the situation and spell it out to the point we see our mistakes. Accepting one thing can be ok, but accepting all the truth about oneself can be a challenge to embrace at one time. Let's go a little deeper into accepting one's situation. We all know that trials and situations come to distract us from moving forward.

What I mean about going deeper is that when it comes to fear, we face failure and how it grips us into being stagnant and paralyzed.

- What is making you paralyzed?
- What is making you feel like you are a failure?
- What handicaps you from living your life with complete fullness?

JOURNAL

Let Us Pray!!

Heavenly Father,

We thank You for your guidance and protection in our lives. We acknowledge Your presence in all we do and recognize Your power to calm our fears and anxieties.

Help us to accept fear as a part of life without allowing it to control us.

Remind us, Lord, that fear can actually be a positive force if it leads us closer to You and pushes us out of our comfort zones.

Strengthen us with courage so that we may face our fears head-on and come out victorious on the other side.

Thank you for giving us the ability to trust in You even when we feel most uncertain about our futures.

Empower us with faith so that we may never be overwhelmed by fear. In Your holy name. Amen.

Step 3

ANALYZING

Every step of your journey is very critical as you progress. You learn more about yourself and how crippled you are in your mind. Accepting that you are aware of your fear can move you forward in the process. However, don't get stuck on just knowing you are in fear. Fear can still come and hinder your progression even when you notice its existence. You must gain the strength to continue and see the results.

Once you accept your fear, it is time to analyze, unlearn and learn. Let's start with analyzing what fear means to you. We have various beliefs about fear. When analyzing fear, you gain your power back by understanding what has been fueling it. For example, someone may believe fear equates to failure, weakness, or even thinking you aren't intelligent enough. However, you determine or define fear. You must understand how it has prevented you from just starting toward your passion.

This was one of the most vulnerable moments in my life. I had to overcome it by analyzing my situation. I saw myself being stuck in a battle of hearsay. What I mean is my fear came due to what men had spoken over me. My heart had grabbed hold of those words; I agreed with them and walked them out. I believed I would never be anything, see the fruit of my labor, or see lives change through my voice. This was my unhealthy and unhelpful belief. It's interesting how people speak over you to cancel out the very thing you are to use to move forward to passionately live your life.

Take a moment to ask yourself the following question:

- What do you fear?
- What scares you?
- What does fear mean to me?
- What belief have I been holding on to when it comes to fear?
- What have I learned about fear and me?
- What is a fear you have that you are ashamed to admit?
- What do you want to accomplish, but haven't because of fear?
- What is my reaction or behavior when I feel fearful or doubtful?
- What has been spoken over me that has hindered my growth of confidence from just starting?

Now that you have analyzed fear, it is key to unlearn unhealthy and unhelpful beliefs! List, from your fears, what belief you would like to unlearn that has kept you from moving forward.

JOURNAL

Let Us Pray!

Loving and Merciful God,

We seek Your guidance and protection in this time of uncertainty. Fear has become so pervasive in our lives, that sometimes it can feel like we can't think or act through difficult decisions without its influence. But you are the one who calms our fears and gives us the courage to move forward with confidence.

Help us to analyze fear when it enters into our lives. Show us how to address any anxiety or worries in a healthy way, rather than allowing them to dictate our decisions and actions. Help us to distinguish between rational fears that protect us and irrational ones that paralyze us from taking action.

Teach us how to use scripture as a weapon against these negative thoughts and feelings. Remind us of Your power and promises, such as:

"Fear not, for I am with you; be not dismayed, for I am your God; I will strengthen you, I will help you, I will uphold you with my righteous right hand." (Isaiah 41:10)

"Even though I walk through the valley of the shadow of death, I will fear no evil, for You are with me;" (Psalm 23:4)

We acknowledge that this process can take time and effort to overcome our fears. Give us the patience to persevere even in times when it seems like we're stuck in a cycle of fear. Provide a way out from those moments when fear seems all-consuming.

Create in us a spirit of courage, so that we may trust You and rely on Your guidance at every step. Give us the wisdom to identify our fears and the strength to address them head-on.

We ask for protection against Satan's schemes and his attempts to keep us in fear and anxiety. Help us remain confident in You, O Lord so that no matter what comes our way, we can stand firm on Your promises, knowing that You are with us always.

Through Jesus Christ, Amen.

$\mathscr{S}tep\ 4$
ANNOUNCING

When it comes to facing fear head-on, after recognizing the root (unhealthy and unhelpful belief), I like to say, "Do it afraid, ANY WAY!", and "I can do hard things!" Because the truth of the matter is, you CAN! However, announcing goes beyond just yelling an affirmation. It is to be a heartfelt confession, not just head knowledge.

Dismantle the unhealthy and defeating belief by taking your power back! 2 Corinthians 10:5 says, "We are destroying sophisticated arguments and every exalted and proud thing that sets itself up against the [true] knowledge of God, and we are taking every thought and purpose captive to the obedience of Christ." The Bible speaks of fear as an obstacle that should not stand in our way of progress. Proverbs 29:25 says, "Fear of man will prove to be a snare, but whoever trusts in the Lord is kept safe."

Here we learn that it is not wise to be driven by fear, because it can cause us to miss out on opportunities or have our dreams go unfulfilled. We should instead rely on the Lord's strength and love so that we can live courageously without any doubts or anxieties hindering us from succeeding.

Fear is a powerful emotion. Nevertheless, it should never control our lives. The Bible speaks about fear many times throughout the scriptures and encourages us to live courageously. We are taught in 2 Timothy 1:7 that God did not give us a spirit of fear, but of power, love and self-discipline. It reminds us that God did not create us with fear but power, love, and self-discipline to take on whatever may come our way.

To delete fear from our lives, we must actively fight against it by believing the promises found in God's word. We must trust Him completely and turn away from those things that bring fear into our lives. Just as Psalm 56:3 says, "When I am afraid, I put my trust in you." With this trust, we can confidently stand against any challenge or obstacle life throws at us and pursue what lies ahead, knowing that nothing can separate us from His love. (Romans 8:39)

God has promised never to leave or forsake us. (Hebrews 13:5) So, when fear attempts to fill our minds with doubt and anxiety, we can rely on Him for strength, courage and peace. Fear will no longer have any control over us if we place our trust in Him and learn to recognize the presence of His loving Spirit within us, which always guides us toward safety and freedom.

Take the time to identify your self-defeating beliefs, and then replace them with truth and love:

Examples of self-defeating beliefs:
- "I can never make a mistake."
- "Others are more important than me."
- "I should always be strong."

Truth and Love Statements:
- "Making mistakes is proof that I am trying."
- "I am just as important as others, and I deserve care also."
- "It is ok to get the help I need. Asking for help is a form of caring for myself."

From the examples, what was the biggest obstacle you faced

when doing this assignment? What is the fear that you hold onto that you don't want to relinquish its power?

JOURNAL

Let's Pray!

Heavenly Father,

We come to You today asking for Your help in overcoming fear. We know that fear is a powerful emotion and can take hold of us if we are not careful. Help us recognize when fear begins to creep into our hearts and minds so that we may confront it with courage and strength. Give us the faith to move forward, despite our fears and doubts.

Help us recognize that You are with us in all things—wherever we go and face, You will be there. Remind us of Your protection so that even when fear tempts us to turn away from You, we may remain rooted in faith and trust.

We thank You for Your never-ending love and guidance, Lord. Help us to face our fears with courage and grace, for You are a fortress of protection. In Jesus' name, we pray, Amen.

Step 5

ACCOMPLISHMENTS

You should be proud of yourself that you have made it this far! Now, it is time to "Re-new and Re-frame"! During the "Re-new and Re-frame" process, we replace negative thoughts that create an unhealthy mental space through thoughts of anxiety, depression, and pain with helpful thoughts. Healthy thoughts create a safe, creative space for your mind to think clearly. Unhealthy thinking creates a sense of perfectionist thinking. This is one of the main reasons someone may remain stuck in procrastination, avoid situations, or never accomplish their goals.

By completing the following assessment by Bill Gaultiere, you will be able to identify the perfectionistic thoughts that trip you up. Make an effort to Re-frame that critical perfectionistic thought with a self-compassion statement.

Assessment

Self-Assessment Perfectionism Screening Test

By Bill Gaultiere © 2000, 2012

Perfectionism is a response to anxiety that can be damaging to your relationships and your performance. The following test can help you assess if you're struggling with perfectionism.

Perfectionism Test

For each question below answer "yes" if it's generally true of you and "no" if it's generally *not* true of you. (You may want to ask a close family or friend to confirm your answers to be sure you're being realistic in your self-assessment.)

1.	Yes	No	I often think that I should've done better than I did.
2.	Yes	No	I tend to put things off if I don't have the time to do them perfectly.
3.	Yes	No	I'm afraid to fail when working on an important project.
4.	Yes	No	I strive to impress others with my best qualities or accomplishments.
5.	Yes	No	I think less of myself if I repeat a mistake.
6.	Yes	No	I strive to maintain control of my emotions at all times.
7.	Yes	No	I get upset when things don't go as planned.
8.	Yes	No	I am often disappointed in the quality of other people's work.
9.	Yes	No	I feel that my standards couldn't be too high.
10.	Yes	No	I'm afraid that people will think less of me if I fail.
11.	Yes	No	I'm constantly trying to improve myself.
12.	Yes	No	I'm unhappy if anything I do is considered average.
13.	Yes	No	My home and office need to be clean and orderly always.
14.	Yes	No	I feel inferior to others who are more intelligent, attractive, or successful than I.
15.	Yes	No	I must look my very best whenever I'm out in public.

Scoring: Five or more yes answers suggest a potential problem with perfectionism. (This is a screening test only. For an accurate diagnoses, consult a qualified professional.)

Now that you have completed the assessment, it should be easy for you to target perfectionistic thoughts.

Examples:

- I am a failure, because I didn't get that project done on time.
- I am a failure, because I couldn't get the project done perfectly.
- I am a failure, because I don't have everything under control.
- I am a failure, because I didn't do as well as my brother at school.

I'm going to give you a few examples of what perfectionistic thinking might look like and how you can reframe it with self-compassion statements.

- I'm going to give you a few examples of what perfectionistic thinking might look like and how you can reframe it with self-compassion statements.

- "I have to do this perfectly." You can reframe that thought with, "I am doing my best, and I am learning from this experience."

- "No one will like what I create." You can reframe that thought with, "Everyone has something to offer the world. No one is perfect, so let me not be so hard on myself!

- Let's say you are working on a project, and you start to think, "I have to make this perfect, or else it will be a waste of time." You could reframe that thought by saying, "I am human, and I will make mistakes no matter how hard I try. It is okay if this project isn't perfect because it will still serve as a learning experience for me."

- A writer is frustrated with a project and is worried that their first draft will not be good enough. So, they feel stuck in procrastinating as they struggle to write their paper. Then the perfectionistic thought might be something like, "I need to write the perfect first draft." But, what if they reframe that thought with a self-compassion statement like, "It is okay to not have everything figured out right now? I am just trying my best and that is enough. It is okay to take my time in learning this new skill!"

No longer will you allow fear of accomplishment hold you back by way of perfectionistic thoughts. You are ready to accomplish something great. The way around it is clear. Instead of avoiding the things you're afraid of, take action toward those things, even when fear comes up. You'll find that God is faithful to give you the strength and courage you need, so don't let fear stop you from doing what He has called you to do! In this scripture example, Abram was obedient, and he stepped out into new territory as he left his family and went toward the place that God had promised him. In another scripture example in Exodus chapter 14, Moses led the children of Israel out of Egypt through the Red Sea as they escaped slavery and bondage. Moses was afraid they would all die on their journey, but he was willing to enter into death if it meant freedom for his people. So, he stepped forward into what he was fearful of to save his people from their bondage.

In both examples, the people were obedient and stepped out into new territory. Sometimes we have to be like Abram, leave our families, and move toward the place God has promised us. When he was told to leave his family behind, he did not question it; he just obeyed and trusted God with his life. We do not know what will happen when we step out into the unknown. We can only trust that God knows what He is doing and that He has a plan for us. When we obey God's will, He will make a way where there seems to be no way. When God told Abram to go to a place he did not know, Abram trusted Him with his life.

JOURNAL

Let US Pray!!

Heavenly Father,

We thank You for the strength to overcome our fears. We are grateful that You have seen fit to be with us through our struggles and triumphs alike. Your loving guidance and support have enabled us to reach milestones in our lives that would otherwise not have been possible.

We give thanks for the courage to face challenges head-on, rather than let fear stand in our way. Through hard work, dedication and determination, we can achieve more than we ever dreamed of – all because of You. Help us continue on this path of progress and never forget why it is so important: to honor Your name!

In Jesus' name, Amen.

Conclusion

The idea of overcoming fear can seem like a monumental task. It's easy to get bogged down in everything that could go wrong or what you might lose if you fail. But break it down, and you'll see that overcoming fear is much easier than it seems. It all starts with acknowledging the fear itself.

It makes sense that you'd be afraid of something as big as stepping out into uncharted territory. Especially when so many other people have been right where you are and failed. Whether their failure was overt—they put their whole heart into something that didn't work out, or it was just a case of them being unable to leap. The fact is that people have tried before, and they've failed. And, they've had the same fears you do now.

When we acknowledge our fears, we don't let them fester and grow. We don't let them control us and hold us back from our goals. The best way to do this is by writing them down or talking about them with someone who cares about your success. It's also important to really think about why you're afraid of something and how you can overcome those obstacles within yourself.

In hindsight, we must know and trust that fear is not from God but from the enemy. God told us to have faith in Him, and we will have no fear of failure, rejection, what others might think of us, or fear of not being accepted by others for who we are. The Bible says that to be free from the fear of man; our focus must be on God and His promises.

However, we must acknowledge the fear is there, analyze the reason for its presence, and then announce to ourselves that we are going to walk in faith instead of fear. While it may not be easy, we can accomplish this in Jesus' name.

If we focus on fear, it will grow and become a monster in our lives. However, as we focus on Jesus and all He has done for us, then we can live in freedom from fear.

References

Psychalive.org. (2023). I see you. I hear you. It is so: The powerful tool of acknowledgment in achieving self actualization. Retrieved from https://www.psychalive.org/i-see-you-i-hear-you-it-is-so-the-powerful-tool-of-acknowledgment-in-achieving-self-actualization/

Medicine.llu.edu. (2023) Self-Assessment Perfectionism Screening Test. Retrieved from https://medicine.llu.edu/sites/medicine.llu.edu/files/docs/self-assessment-perfectionism-test.pdf